GETTING
SOCIAL
SECURITY
DISABILITY

Your 9 Step Individual Action Plan

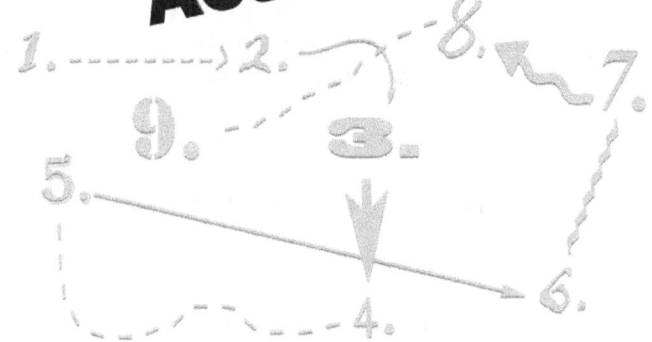

Loretta Crosby

Getting Social Security Disability: Your 9 Step Individual Action Plan

Visit us online at www.OnePupilPublications.com

ISBN-13: 978-1463713393

ISBN-10: 1463713398

One Pupil Publications
Gastonia NC 28056

Cover and Book Design by Cynthia Mulligan

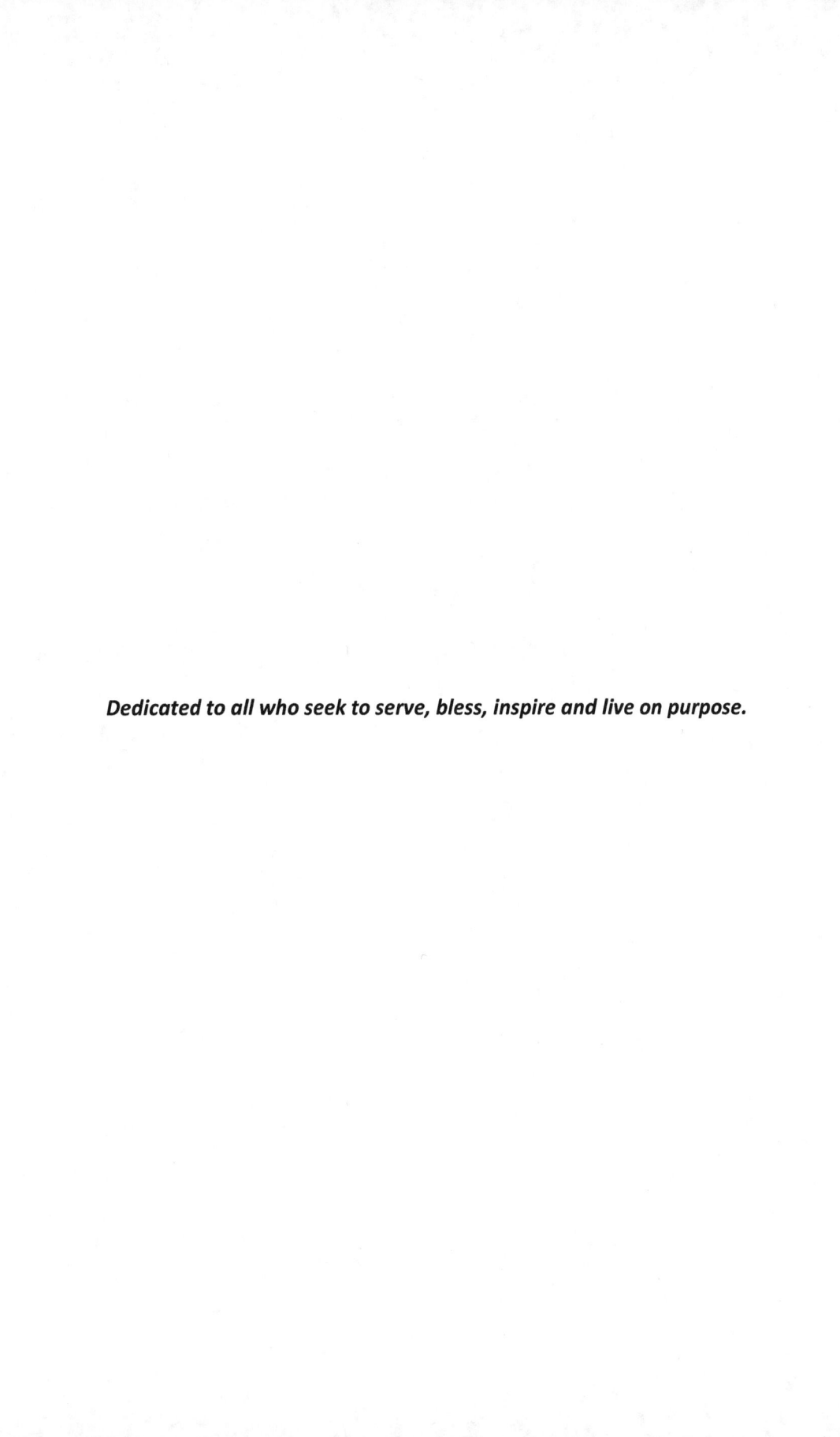

Dedicated to all who seek to serve, bless, inspire and live on purpose.

CONTENTS

"The hardest years in life are those between ten and seventy."
Helen Hayes

.

INTRODUCTION

If you have a disability or a severe impairment that prevents you from working, and your impairment is expected to last at least a year, or is terminal, then you may be eligible for Social Security Disability Insurance (SSDI) and/or Supplemental Security Income (SSI) benefit assistance from the federal government.

Both programs are administered by the Social Security Administration (SSA) through its contracts with state Disability Determination Services (DDS) or Disability Adjudication Services' (DAS) offices.

At these state agencies, disability examiners (DEs) coordinate, gather and collect information needed to make a medical and vocational decision on your claim. In close collaboration with Medical Consultants (physicians, medical specialists and psychologists), they issue a decision on whether you do or do not qualify for benefits based on the policies, rules and regulations set forth by the SSA.

Role of the Social Security Administration (SSA) Field Office in Disability Claims

The SSA Field Office is the local office of the SSA, which initially accepts your application for disability benefits. This office verifies your identity, determines if you meet certain financial and other requirements, and determines if you qualify to apply for SSDI and/ or SSI benefits. All areas of your application, with the exception of deciding whether you are vocationally or medically disabled, are managed by the Field Office. If you pass this screening process, your application is then forwarded to your state DDS or DAS office to determine your medical eligibility for benefits.

Role of the Disability Examiner (DE) and the Medical Consultant (MC) in the Disability Determination Process

The disability examiner or claims examiner is the person who handles and manages your claim at the DDS office. This is the person who you can call to get updates on your claim status, or the person who might call you if there is any missing information on your application.

In most cases, after all necessary information is collected by the disability examiner, your medical records are then summarized by the examiner handling your claim, and routed to one or more medical consultant(s) for review. If you are alleging a physical disability, it will be routed to a medical doctor who might or might not hold a specialty. If you are alleging a mental disability, your claim will be summarized and routed to a psychologist for review. Or, if you are alleging a combination of both physical and mental impairments, your claim will go to both of these medical consultants, and each will enter his/her findings separately.

Medical consultants – which include medical doctors, physicians, specialists or psychologists-- serve as direct staff to or contract with the state Disability Determination Services (DDS). They are usually housed in the DDS offices. A Medical Consultant will either handle claims of all examiners assigned to a particular unit, or they will review claims agency-wide, based on their specialty.

Their duty is to use their professional expertise in determining the extent of a claimant's functional ability in light of his or her medical condition(s). These doctors and psychologists never see you in person so they must rely solely on your medical records (MER) in file to assess your limitations.

After a review of the summary provided by the claims examiner and your medical records, the medical consultant (MC) will either concur with the disability examiner or revise the summary findings based on their judgment. In some cases, they will send the case back to the examiner and request that he or she collect further medical information, or they may require the results of certain medical tests or psychological assessments be performed before they issue a final assessment on your functional abilities.

When the medical consultants have completed their review of your file, the case is then forwarded back to the disability examiner who then assesses your vocational/work history. Based on the level of your restrictions as determined by the physician or psychologist, the disability examiner looks at your past work history to determine whether you can or cannot return to your past work. If your medical restrictions indicate that you cannot, based on the specific requirements of that type work, the examiner then has to determine if you can do any other type of work, based on your age, educational level and physical and/or psychological limitations.

If it is determined that you cannot do your past job or other work, your disability claim will be "allowed". If you can do your past work or can do other work, or it is determined that your disability is not severe or not expected to last at least a year or that your severe condition will resolve itself in less than a year, then your claim will be "denied."

Two Disability Program–An Insurance Program and a Needs-Based Program

While SSDI (Title 2 or regular Social Security Disability Insurance) and SSI (Title 16 or regular Supplemental Security Income) programs have many of the same eligibility requirements, one main difference between the two programs is that the SSDI program is an insurance program and the payouts are based on your past earnings, while the SSI program is a needs based program for those with low or no income and resources, but who otherwise meet the SSA eligibility requirements for medical and / or vocational disability.

The SSDI program is based on your earnings within a certain period prior to application and that makes it extremely important for you to apply for benefits as soon as you determine that you are disabled and can no longer work.

What to Expect from This Guide

The federal disability program's rules and regulations are complex, and this 9 Step Guide does not attempt to explain any of them in detail. There are some excellent resources already out there that will be a good start if you are looking to get an overall picture of the general rules and regulations of the disability programs from start to finish. One of my favorite layman's book is listed in the Resource section under the "Recommended Reading" heading.

The 9 Step Guide's only intent is to give you information on how claims examiners might approach and process claims received in the Disability Determination Services office or the Disability Adjudication Services state offices.

The overall goal of this 9 Step Guide is to help you, as an applicant (or advocate / representative) know what key things to focus on in the presentation of your claim for SS disability or SSI benefits.

If you keep in mind that claims examiners determine whether you are medically and/or vocationally able to engage in "substantial gainful activity" (i.e. work), then you will have to conclude that the focus is almost exclusively on your medical records presented, and next on the determination of how your medical and / or psychological challenges impact your ability to function or not function in a work environment.

When it is all said and done, you will discover that medical records are at the heart of any claim. Your vocational work history is secondary, but becomes extremely important as your age increases because if your condition is severe, then examiners must determine whether you can return to your previous work, or if you can do other work, or if your impairments preclude you from doing any work.

As you age, the likelihood of adjusting to other work decreases so older individuals are much more likely to receive disability benefits as a result of their impairments.

Finally, this Guide only discusses adult disability claims, not children's disability claims. And it by design makes no mention of the first hurdle of the disability application process that happens in the Social Security Administration's field offices which determine your financial or resource eligibility for disability programs.

It only highlights the general processes, which take place in the Disability Determination Services or Disability Adjudication Services offices where the actual decisions are made on a claim.

It is noted that while the processes may change in terms of how claims examiners collect information, the focus on what is needed to prove your disability essentially remains constant.

As an example, while the writer served as an examiner in two state DDS offices, where claims were handled manually and medical records came in through the mail, today, records are received online for the most part. However, that change does not affect how examiners are trained to approach and adjudicate disability claims.

So information shared in this Guide could prove useful for disability applicants, their advocates, representatives and attorneys for many years to come.

Online Access

As you go through the Steps, you will notice certain words and phrases are underlined. These are hyperlinks which have been held over from the eBook version of this publication. They have been deliberately left in so you can access the information online should you choose to do so. Visit: http://9steps2disability.com/hyperlink-resources.html to view the additional information associated with the underlined word(s).

DICTIONARY OF DISABILITY TERMS

(As used in this Guide and / or internally at the DDS Office)

Allowance: This refers to any disability claim that has been processed, evaluated and approved for benefits.

CE: Consultative Examination. This is a medical exam set up by the disability claims examiner for applicants whose medical records do not contain all of the pertinent information or testing that is necessary to reach a decision on their claims.

DAS or DDS Office: Disability Adjudication Services or Disability Determination Services offices. These are state agencies that contract with the Social Security Administration to provide assessment of a claimant's current medical condition and vocational history, and to make a determination as to whether a claimant is or is not disabled from doing work based on that assessment using SSA rules, policies and regulations.

DE: Disability Examiners or Claims Examiners. DEs coordinate the gathering of all medical and vocational information necessary to reach a decision on a claim based on SSA policies and regulations.

They work in collaboration with Medical Consultants (MC) who are charged with determining a claimant's "residual functioning capacity", i.e. what a claimant can still do or not do based on their particular medical impairment(s).

DEs generally write up a case summary on each claim after all the medical records and vocational history has been received, and then submits the medical summary to the medical consultant for review.

Once the medical consultant has determined what the claimant can or cannot still do "functionally" based on their medical condition, the claim is returned to the DE who then provides a vocational assessment which will indicate if the claimant can return to his past job, can do other work or cannot do any other work in the national economy.

To make this vocational determination, DEs refer to the Dictionary of Occupational Titles (DOT) and the work history form the claimant completes at application to see what specific functions are required for any jobs the claimant has had in the past 15 years.

The DE then inputs a claims decision into the computer, either "allowing" or "denying" a claim, and returns the claim back to the Social Security Field Office (FO) for final processing, including notifying the claimant of the decision.

The claim decision will sometimes be intercepted and reviewed, at random, by an internal quality review team before it leaves the DDS office. If this happens, the case will either be returned to the DE for further processing if something is found to be out of order, or it will be sent on to the FO for final processing.

Denial: This refers to any claim that has been denied benefits.

FO: The Field Office is the local branch of the Social Security Administration's office in a particular locality. The FO accepts applications for disability and determines eligibility on all aspects of the claim, with the exception of the medical and vocational assessment.

If a claimant meets all the other requirements for disability, the FO forwards the claim to the DDS office so they can determine if a claimant is totally disabled either medically or vocationally.

MC: Medical Consultants are either Disability Determination Services' in house staff or they contract with DDS to provide "paper" assessments on the severity of a claimant's physical or psychological impairments. Generally, MCs are housed at the DDS office, whether they contract with DDS or are on DDS payroll.

Medical Consultants are physicians and psychologists, and other specialist doctors such as internists, ophthalmologists, oncologists, optometrists, etc.

Their role is to review the medical information in file on a claimant and to translate that information into a decision as to what the claimant is still able to do or not do based on the medical condition(s) documented in the case record.

They, in effect, determine the claimant's "residual functioning capacity", i.e. what a claimant can or cannot do based on their medical condition. Ideally, medical consultants would review all the medical information in a claimant's file, but in practice, they usually review and sign off on a case summary that is written up by a disability claims examiner, who is generally not a doctor.

The more experienced the disability examiner is, the more thorough the case summary tends to be, i.e. the less they will leave out pertinent information necessary for a fair assessment by the MC.

Medical consultants have the power to send a case back to the examiner for the purpose of gathering additional information on a claimant's medical condition if they feel that there is not enough information in file to make an assessment on a claimant's functional limitations, or if they feel that certain other tests need to be performed prior to their assessment.

MER: Medical Evidence of Record. This refers to any medical information that is received and in file on a claimant during the disability determination process.

SSA: The Social Security Administration. This federal agency administers the Social Security Disability Insurance (SSDI) and the

Supplemental Security Income (SSI) programs. It usually contracts with a state agency to provide disability determinations through agencies such as the DDS office or DAS office, via state Vocational Rehabilitation departments.

TP: Treating Physician. This refers to a claimant's regular treating doctor, i.e. the doctor that should have the most complete records on a claimant's current medical condition and history.

TPs sometimes provide letters of support for a claimant's allegation of disability. The opinions of the treating physician is always given more weight than the opinion of a consultative exam (CE) doctor, but *only* if the TP cites the specific medical or subjective evidence in the claimant's medical records that forms the basis for his or her conclusions.

YOUR 9 STEP
INDIVIDUAL ACTION PLAN

Many people who apply for Social Security Disability or SSI benefits are subsequently denied for various reasons, or their claim may take a long time to process. This Individual Action Plan for Getting Social Security Disability or SSI benefits provides you with a list of nine things you can do to help you get an accurate disability decision in the least amount of time.

By following these steps, you should experience less stress throughout the process, and you should have the best chance of getting a favorable decision on your claim.

STEP 1:
PREPARE YOURSELF MENTALLY

Three of the main stressors associated with applying for Social Security Disability or SSI benefits are:

1. A fear of the unknown,
2. The amount of time it takes to get a decision, and
3. The anticipation that your application will be denied, no matter how disabled you are.

So let's take a look at these stressors individually.

The best way to conquer the fear of dealing with this governmental program is to learn all you can about the process. This Individual Action Plan (IAP) should arm you with the basic things you need to know, and to become comfortable with, in order to successfully navigate the bureaucratic maze.

Sometimes a decision on your claim can take a long time, due to either overburdened DDS office staff or other reasons. And this translates into a very long time when you are no longer working and your bills continue to pile up. There is no easy solution to the problem of lack of money unless you have savings to draw on while you wait, or have family members who can "carry" you until your claim is decided.

One solution to this problem is to apply for other state or local aid programs that you may be entitled to while you wait. This may involve applying for Food Stamps or Aid to Families with Dependent Children (which may operate under a different name in your state, i.e. Department of Social Services, Department of Family and Children Services, etc.) The latter, if you are eligible, usually comes with medical benefits (Medicaid) as well as financial assistance payments.

In both of these situations, you will be "living off the fat of the land", as some would call it. That is not an entirely bad thing, especially considering that while you were working and paying taxes, you contributed to those programs so that others in your situation could benefit.

If you are a person who has a lot of pride or feels shameful in requesting assistance from other people or government agencies, having to ask for a hand can be stressful all by itself. The best thing to do is: lose your pride, and check your shame ticket at the door before you enter this new world. Having pride can serve you well in many different areas of your life. This is not one of them, so the sooner you release it, the smoother will be the process.

The third stressor may be your anticipation that even if you are patient and wait, that your final decision will be a denial of benefits. Many people are denied benefits when they first apply for disability benefits so this *might* not just be an unfounded general fear. Still, it might be unfounded in your particular case so your job is to believe that your application for benefits will be approved. Period.

The best way to deal with the additional stressors that you may experience while seeking disability benefits is to prepare yourself for the process mentally. To do this, you must have a way to get centered daily. Here are five things you might do.

1. Meditation is one way to do this. If you already have a system you use. Great. If not, <u>Bill Harris at Centerpointe</u> can introduce you to meditation in a way that can easily be integrated into your current lifestyle. If you can listen to a CD with headphones on, then you can use his system to relax yourself and calm yourself daily. (I credit it with helping me to get crucial things done, as well, like completing this Guide):-

2. Visualization is another way to reduce the stress of it all. As it relates to your disability claim, you might try visualizing being successful with your claim. For example: close your eyes and visually see that first check coming in the mail (or being deposited into your checking account). There is power in being able to see, and more importantly to feel, that a thing already exists before it actually does exist.

3. Talk to family members or friends about what's on your mind. You can often gain a fresh perspective when you discuss your fears and concerns with others.

4. If you know someone who works or has worked in governmental programs or services, talk to him or her about the specific requirements and what to expect. If you do not know someone personally, read this Plan in its entirety.

5. Lastly--and this is important--if you have a mental impairment or mental disability, go ahead and find yourself a friend, family member or disability advocate who will work with Social Security Disability agencies on your behalf.

   One place to start would be your church or religious organization, if you are a part of one. The members may know someone there or know of someone there or elsewhere who knows how to navigate the system.

If you have been hospitalized, many hospitals will have in house social workers whose job it is to know how to assist claimants with navigating the disability system. They are often anxious to assist because if you are successful with your claim, the hospital has a better chance of being paid.

But, regardless of whom you get to assist you, do try to find someone. If you think you do not need a representative, it might just be your mental condition speaking to you. Do not listen to it. And if you still think you do not need a representative, get one anyway, if only for the impression it will send to your disability examiner, i.e. "This claimant cannot even handle the simple thing of applying for benefits" on their own. This can only help your mental disability claim.

Action Step #1: Do what you have to do to reduce the amount of stress in your life during the disability examination process. What is going to happen will happen. Your task is not to let any of it get you down. You are alive. You have worth, and you are loved.

STEP 2:
COMPLETE YOUR ADULT DISABILITY APPLICATION FORM WITH A FOCUS ON FUNCTION

Now what does that mean, exactly? It means you need to begin to see your disability or impairment with an eye on demonstrating how it affects your ability to do (or not do) the basic requirements of your past job or any job within the national economy.

When You Allege a Physical Disability or Impairment

Physical functional capacity includes things like: can you sit, stand, stoop, bend, squat, etc.? How long can you sit, stand, stoop, bend, squat? Can you do any lifting? How much can you lift?

These questions are all found on the work history form, which you either completed with your initial application or will be asked to complete when your claim reaches the Disability Determination Services office.

Many applicants will gloss over completing the work history form because they do not want to take the time to calculate how long they stood or sat during their 8-hour work shift. This is a huge mistake because those items speak directly to what you had to do to "function" on your job.

If your job required you to lift 20 pounds consistently and your new heart condition or your spinal problems cause you to be able to only lift 5-10 pounds occasionally, then you clearly can no longer meet the physical requirements of your last job. If that is the case, then you have just jumped over several major hurdles in the disability determination process if it is decided that your medical condition is a severe one that is expected to last at least a year.

When You Allege a Mental Disability or Impairment

Of course, with a mental impairment, you may be able to perform all of the above purely physical work requirements, but there are other basic requirements needed to be "mentally capable" of holding a job.

For example:

- Can you remember locations and work procedures?
- Can you understand and remember very short and simple instructions and carry them out?
- Are you capable of remembering detailed instructions and implementing them?
- Can you maintain attention and concentration for short or extended periods of time?
- Can you perform activities within a schedule, maintain regular attendance and be punctual within customary tolerances?
- Can you work around others?
- Can you manage an everyday routine without special supervision?
- Can you make simple work related decisions?
- Can you accept supervision?
- Can you maintain behaviors socially appropriate in the workplace, including basic cleanliness and neatness of appearance?
- Are you able to respond appropriately to changes in the work setting?

These questions and others regarding your mental abilities are answered by your disability examiner based on information in your file if you are alleging a mental disability, and that disability has been determined by your claims examiner to be severe.

Keep these basic requirements in mind, on your tongue and in your writing as you complete your application, and use those "function" words in describing your limitations.

For example, if you suffered from a mental impairment, you might write:

"I have difficulty working around others because they always plot against me."

Sources Used to Determine Your Current Functioning Level

Disability examiners determine your level of functioning from various sources, including medical reports and tests, psychological assessments and tests, work histories, together with information gathered from third parties such as your friends and family members, counselors, social workers, employers, psychologists and even school records, if applicable.

Sometimes your claim will be assessed for a mental disability even though you have not alleged a mental impairment. Keep in mind that on all claims where a person has had a history of special education classes in school that that claim will have to be assessed for a mental impairment as well.

If this is the case with your claim -- where you have had a history of special education -- but you have not had any mental health problems or mental health providers, the claims examiner will at a minimum send out an "Activities of Daily Living" form to you or to someone who knows you, in an effort to gather enough information to determine if any presumed mental impairment can be dismissed as non-severe. Based on this information, the examiner will also decide whether a psychological exam might be needed to further assess the extent of any mental limitations.

Function Reports and Activities of Daily Living Report Forms

In most cases, if you receive an "adult function report" to complete, it means that your claim is being assessed for a mental impairment either singularly or in combination with a physical impairment.

Two obvious things that will trigger an examiner to assess your claim for a mental disability even if you do not allege a mental impairment are:

1. If you have listed a prescription medication that is a known psychotropic drug (i.e. drugs that are capable of affecting the mind or those used to treat psychiatric disorders such as anxiety, depression, schizophrenia, etc.). Two such drugs that come immediately to mind are Prozac and the generic Amitriptyline, a widely prescribed antidepressant.
2. If you have indicated a history of special education in elementary, middle of high school on your initial application form, your claim will include a mental assessment.

   With collateral sources, such as your spouse, friend or other family members who may be asked to fill out an "Activities of Daily Living" (ADL) questionnaire, they can help you by realizing what the form is trying to assess. This section also pertains to the Adult Function Report form that you might be asked to complete.

   For example, the section on the ADL form that asks about money used to read something like this:

   > "Are you able to pay bills? Count change, handle a savings account, use a checkbook/money orders."

   Some claimants will just indicate "N/A", meaning that they are not able to pay bills, do not have a savings account, etcetera, because they do not have money to pay their bills right now due to no income coming into the home. However, these questions are only trying to access whether you *would be* able to pay bills or handle a checking account given your current mental level.

The questions are not concerned with whether you have money in the bank, as many claimants presume. Remember, you have already passed the income/resource requirement to qualify for benefits or your claim would not have made it to the DDS office. The DDS office is only concerned with determining your mental and/or physical functioning level, in combination with your work/vocational history, age and educational level.

What most of the questions on the function report and ADL reports are trying to assess is, "*Does this claimant still retain the mental capacity to do this or that task, to function in this or that work environment?*"

To take it a step further, the examiner is trying to see clearly what your "residual functioning level" is despite your impairment, to decide if you are still able to do or not do work based on your current mental functioning level.

Therefore, if you have a form in front of you that you have been asked to complete, focus on completely answering all questions that hint to mental capacities, as that is the primary purpose of this ADL form.

It has been my experience that physical disabilities can more easily be assessed through medical exams. Mental impairments are more subjective, so the examiner has to rely on what your psychologist, counselors, friends and family members say or observe about you.

On form 3373, if that is the one you receive to tell about your functioning, there is a section C entitled "*Information about Abilities*". Examiners pay particular attention if the boxes are checked which indicate problems with memory, completing tasks, concentration, and understanding, following instructions and getting along with others. One cannot hold a job if you have significant problems in any of these areas.

Medications and Dosages

Additionally, the dosage and strength of any prescription medications you list on your initial application are reviewed thoroughly by the examiner. This helps DEs determine how well you can function in a work environment. So be sure to indicate this piece of information on your application or update your application if you neglected to include it.

While a small number of people will indicate that it is the side effects of the medications that are rendering them disabled, please know that examiners have no training in assessing side effects so they are rarely if ever considered when they summarize your case findings, unless your treating doctor has taken the time to list it as a symptom in his case notes.

What examiners can determine from your psychotropic medications is whether you are taking a dosage that "half of the people in America" are taking, or whether you are on a higher dose. Many people are on Prozac or antidepressants. What will determine if your mental condition is more than non-severe is the dosage of these medications, so you should indicate the dosage as well as how often you are required to take the medication in a given day.

Other Factors Affecting Your Functioning: Age, Education, Work Skill and Exertional Levels

The SSA considers your age, your education, work skill and work exertional levels for the past 15 years in assessing your functioning ability. With age, it is determined that the older you are, the more unlikely it is that you will be able to adjust to a new job if it has been determined that you can no longer do your old job due to your impairment.

Educational level is a factor too as you advance in age. An older person who only completed a middle school level education will have more difficulty in finding new work if they can no longer do their old job. It may be harder for them to learn new skills if they did not complete high school or do not have a GED.

In fact, the SSA has a GRID chart that lists all these factors so that once the examiner has completed the forms indicating your residual functioning level, he can then look on the GRID chart which will tell him whether or not you are to be found disabled or not. But, the GRID rules are only applicable for claims alleging a physical disability.

What that means is that after all the medical information is gathered, the vocational information is gathered (which tells whether you did sedentary, light, medium or heavy level work), your educational level is noted, and then the GRID rules will indicate whether your case is allowed or denied.

While that may seem mechanical, it means that the examiners do not have to use their own judgment in the final decision because a finding of disabled or not disabled is in fact mandated by SSA through the use of the GRIDS.

Best to Focus on Function in Completing Your Application

By focusing on what basic work related activities you can no longer do as a result of your disability, you have a greater chance of giving your disability examiner information s/he can use in accurately assessing the extent of your impairments.

Because disability examiners and medical consultants who review your claim never see you, your job is to make it clear on paper what things you can and cannot do which has been listed in the basic work requirements as noted in this Step. You job is to paint a picture of what you were able to do prior to your disability versus what you can no longer do now.

In disability examinations, *function is everything*. In reality, examiners are not looking at whether or not you have a recent diagnosis of HIV or AIDS. You could be asymptomatic with no functional limitations as a result of this or that diagnosis, in which case your claim will be denied.

Keep in mind that this is used only as an example, because, if by chance your diagnosis is listed in the SSA "blue book" as one that will cause a claims "allowance", then you would be granted benefits. The Blue Book is updated periodically, so the exact diagnoses that indicate an allowance are subject to change from time to time.

Diagnoses as a Factor in Claim Decision

Having said that, you should know that diagnosis alone could be a factor in deciding your claim, so you should clearly state what diagnoses the doctor has given you on your application. While diagnosis is something you have no control over, if your claim application lists that you have chronic renal failure with weekly kidney dialysis, it can clue the examiner to the fact that this claim can be expedited for immediate approval, as this is a diagnosis that is listed in the SSA's blue book of impairments which examiners refer to for fast claim allowances / approvals. The same would hold true for cases alleging certain types of metastatic cancers. So be sure to list your diagnoses together with any specific related details on your initial application.

Action Step 2: Write a statement / paragraph explaining why you are disabled from working. (In Step 5 of this guide there is a sample statement written in the language of function. After you have read the sample, feel free to come back and revise your statement.) A good place to put this statement is on your application form 3368* -- www.ssa.gov/online/ssa-3368.pdf. The question on the form is worded as below:

How do your illnesses, injuries, or conditions limit your ability to work?

Note: if you had a job that you are no longer able to do, the question you really want to answer instead is this one:

How do your illnesses, injuries, or conditions limit your ability to function on your job? Your examiner needs the answer to that question. Please write your answer below.

STEP 3:
STRATEGICALLY CALL THE EXAMINER TO CHECK THE STATUS OF YOUR CLAIM

Periodically checking the status of your disability claim is vital to getting a faster decision on your claim. This section discusses when you should check the status, why you need to check the status and how to check the status. A version of this section is posted in full on _Social-Security-Disability-ESP.com_ because it is so essential to getting a faster decision, so it is reprinted here.

Why Check The Status of Your Disability Application?

Checking the status of your disability claim at the right time can be crucial in helping you speed up processing of your application.

This is because when you call in to get a status check, it forces the disability examiner to take a look at your folder or electronic record, and s/he can then tell you what else is needed for processing, or at least where the claim is in the sequence of steps that are involved in its development.

When Should You Check the Status of Your Disability Claim?

Having worked as a disability examiner, here are my suggestions for when you should check the status of your claim based on the various case development stages of adult initial claims.

1. **You should call your disability examiner (DE) in the state Disability Determination Services (DDS) office or the Disability Adjudication Services (DAS) office 30 days after you have completed your application**. If everything has gone as it should, by then the DE has written to all the doctors/hospitals listed on your application to request your "medical evidence of record" or MER (as it is called internally). The examiner has given these medical providers two to three weeks to get the records turned in. Because the worker makes these requests within days of receiving a new claim for processing, all of your MER should have been received in the first 30 days if your doctors/hospitals staff and their medical records departments have been cooperative in sending the records in to the DDS office.

> *Medical records are the backbone of your claim. If there is no medical evidence to support your claim, you really have no claim, and your claim will be denied. The DE can set up a consultative examination (CE), which allows you to see one of Social Security's participating doctors so that he or she can do a medical exam to provide the missing information. But the bottom line is that the more medical records the examiner has to review, the easier it is to prove your claim for disability based on objective medical findings.*

Unfortunately, most DDS offices have a list (either in writing or in fact) of medical facilities that are notorious for either not providing medical records in a timely matter (if at all) or providing records that have been known to be totally useless in giving the information necessary to decide a claim.

In my experience, medical records from the Veterans Administration, while usually voluminous, generally have little substance unless there are x-rays or other objective test results located in the file.

> *Some states send out second notices automatically to medical providers who fail to respond to a first request for records, and this system helps the examiner tremendously because the first notice may have been misplaced, lost in the mail, etc. North Carolina is one state that did not do this as a matter of course while I served there, so the chances are that your medical records may be incomplete if you do not follow-up. Of course, the examiners are expected to make this follow up request manually, but this may or may not happen depending on how many cases the claims examiner may be managing at any one time.*

So to recap, the reasons you are checking the status of your claim at day-30 is to ask the DE:

A) *"What is the status of my claim?"*
If the worker says something like "It is still pending." or "No decision has been made," then your next question will be:

B) *"Have you gotten my medical records from all of my doctors/hospitals/providers?"*
If they tell you that one or more doctors has not sent in records, then you should

C) *Ask for the names of the doctors or hospitals that have not provided records to date.* Then,

D) *You should, if you are able to or have someone who can, offer to assist the DE in getting those missing medical records.* How?

How You Can Assist the Claims Examiner in Getting Medical Records

You can place a call in to your doctor's office and explain that you have applied for disability and the claims office (DDS of DAS) is waiting to receive records from their facility. Tell the doctors' office – in larger medical facilities, you would be speaking to someone in their "medical records department" – the date the DDS requested the records. (The date the examiner requested the records can easily be gotten from the DE during you first 30-day status check telephone call).

Then ask your doctor or medical facility to, if they are able, fax the information in to the DDS, explaining that it has already been three weeks since the date of the initial request. If they are not able to fax, then try to get a commitment from them that they will mail the records in within the next few days, or send them electronically. Then, you should follow up with your medical provider after a few days to see if they have done it.

In one of the states that I handled disability claims, it was the stated policy of the agency that the DE would not request assistance from claimants in obtaining medical records in SSI claims. I do not know the full logic behind that rule. Still you should know that the more current objective medical records that the DE has to evaluate, the clearer it becomes as to the degree of your functional abilities or disabilities, so if you are applying for SSI, and are able, you should also offer to assist the DE in getting medical records.

E) *When you do your 30-day status check on your claim, and the DE tells you that s/he has received all the MER from all the doctors / hospitals you listed, ask if anything else is needed before s/he can issue a decision.*

If the examiner responds that s/he are also waiting on you to return anything that was sent to you, such as a questionnaire or if s/he says they are waiting to receive an ADL (activity of daily living) form from your aunt Mary or whoever else you listed as a person who knows about your condition, then you should follow up with your aunt Mary to ask her if she has received the form and encourage her to complete it and return it as soon as possible.

Note: Again, depending on the state you live in and apply for benefits, how the DE collects information may vary. In GA, adjudicators were trained primarily to collect info via questionnaires sent to you; in NC, the DEs may prefer to call you for the information. Regardless of the method, your job is to check to be sure the examiner has gotten the information requested from your doctors, hospitals, psychologist, counselors, friends, spouses or any other third parties.

If the information is not received from your treating doctors, from you or from your third parties, the DE will not have the time (or the inclination) to do follow-up and baby sit any party to the claim. They will merely move on to the next step in development, because contrary to popular notion, DEs are evaluated for timeliness in case processing, and begging for MER from a non-cooperating doctor will only slow the process down. So you can be sure that if you are not working to obtain the missing records, chances are that your DE is not working on getting the records either.

Finally, during your 30-day status check call, after you have asked if all the medical records have been received, and if all questionnaires have been received, and if the answer is yes, then you can ask the DE if s/he has had a chance to review your claim or write it up. (DEs in most states are charged with summarizing your case record to be reviewed by in house medical consultants, i.e. physicians or psychologists).

The answer may be "No." If the claims examiner says "I need to review your record to see if any additional information or tests are needed," tell them that that is fine, and then ask, "When can I call back to see if anything else is needed?"

Note: In the ideal world, after all MER and questionnaires are received, the DE would immediately proceed to reviewing all of your medical records, then write up a case summary for review by the staff medical doctor and/or psychologist for concurrence (depending on whether you alleged a physical impairment, a mental impairment or both).

However, because the DDS offices are often understaffed, a case may end up getting no action on it for months after all your information has been received. Your phone call to the DE can trigger such a review and if you promise the DE worker that you will call back in two weeks for an updated status, this action may cause him/her to make a note to review your case before those two weeks are up.

This is done primarily because getting calls from claimants and having to explain why no action has been taken is sometimes harder than going ahead and reviewing and summarizing the case and putting it in the medical consultants' cue for review, especially if the worker can see that the case is going to be a denial.

Cases that look as though they will be a denial often sit on an examiners desk the longest, while approvals and allowances are generally processed first by an examiner.

Some Disability Examiners have the designation as certified "Single Decision Makers" which means that in some types of physical disability cases, they can make the final decision on a claim without any feedback from a medical consultant (staff physician). If this is the case with your claim, you could have a decision within two weeks of such an initial status check phone call.

Claims alleging only a physical disability might not have to be forwarded to a medical consultant for review if your examiner is experienced, and while this may speed up the processing of your claim, it should be noted that one disadvantage to you as a claimant is that if an examiner--who is generally not a medical doctor--makes the final decision on your claim without input from a licensed medical doctor, then you can see how that might not be in your best interest.

2) **Checking the status of your disability claim 45 days after application**.

Depending on what was needed after your first 30-day check, this will determine what questions you will ask during your second or 45-day follow-up. When you call, you can ask:

  i. **"Have all the MER (medical records) now been received?"** If so, "When can I expect a decision?" The DE will generally explain what remains to be done in the process. If s/he does not, you can ask directly, **"What remains to be done in the processing of my claim?"**

  ii. **"Have all the questionnaires now been received?"**

  iii. **"Have you reviewed the record to determine if other MER will be needed?"** The answer to this question is critical. At day 45, it is crucial that a review of your case by the examiner be initiated if you want to ensure you get a decision within 90 days, which is the average time (nationwide) that most claimants receive a decision.

 a) So if at this point you as the claimant report that you have been back to the doctor, know that the DE is obligated to request those new records, which will begin the MER timelines all over again and will make it very difficult to get a decision on your claim in a reasonable amount of time. So if you have been to the doctor for a routine visit where no new tests were done and no new diagnoses were made that changed your ability to function, you might want to K.I.T.Y. the information at that point (Keep It To Yourself)—Hey did I just coin a new term? :) - Keep reading to see when is the most opportune time to report any new medical records you may have.

b) So, if all the MER is in, you can ask the worker whether they will be setting up a consultative examination, (CE) based on the MER in file. Of course, you don't really care how the DE responds to this question because your goal in the 45 day follow-up is to keep the ball rolling so that your claim comes out of the back log stack and moves into the "this claimant will be calling so I better take some action" stack.

c) The goal of asking about a Consultative Exam appointment is to get the examiner to take a look at or at least do a cursory review of your claim to determine if a CE is needed. If it is needed, and depending on which state you are in, you can add another 30 to 75 days to your processing time. That is because the scheduling department will have to arrange for the appointment with a participating medical doctor or psychologist or other physician specialist, and this appointment is then mailed to you and to the doctor. Your consultative examination appointments may be scheduled two weeks later or two months later, depending on the availability of doctors, and whether or not a specialist was needed.

Your 45-day status check has as its primary purpose to:

1) Force the claims DE to do a brief or in-depth review of your claim for the purpose of deciding what further development is needed, and

2) Force the claims DE to begin the process of setting up a doctor's appointment (CE) if not enough MER to "allow" the claim (i.e. issue a favorable decision) has been received, either because your doctor has not sent in your records or because you simply have not had the necessary testing done which can prove your claim, such as x-rays or mental health counseling records, etc.)

3) **After the 45-day status check, you should check on the status of your claim at day 60, and every 15 days thereafter.**

The exception would be if you have been given a consultative examination (CE) doctor's appointment. If a CE has been scheduled and you have attended the examination, there is nothing the worker will be doing on your claim except waiting to receive the results of the examination. So in that case, plan to check the status 15 to 30 days after the date of your CE doctor's visit. (In NC, you might check after 15 days; in GA, wait at least 30 days). Different states allow the medical doctors who conduct your consultative exams different time frames in which to get the results back in to the DDS office. (Note that these timelines may be shorter now with the advent of on line records).

Because you will have to wait for the CE appointment and the results of the exam, this would be an excellent time to inform your claims DE of any other medical records out there that you did not report on your initial application for disability benefits. If you have been back to the doctor, this is the time to let your worker know. That way, they can request them and all the records can be available for review after the CE exam results have been received.

4) **If it has been 30 days after your CE exam, you can be justified in requesting an update on your claim status on a**

weekly basis, unless your DE tells you otherwise. For instance, after the doctor that Social Security sent you to for the examination sends the report to your claims examiner, most will summarize the case and write it up for review by the staff medical consultant as quickly as possible. The only exception would be if the DE is managing a huge caseload and is behind in their work. So,

a. *Your weekly call after you have waited 30 days after a consultative examination* will help get your case in the top of the review piles. This is a case where the squeaky wheel gets the oil because no adjudicator/examiner wants weekly calls on a case that has the results of a consultative examination in file and is ready for a decision. And

b. *When you should not call weekly?* Because the DE knows the workflow of its medical consultants who have to review cases after they have summarized them, ask the examiner the anticipated wait time. The examiner may know that their psych MC has a three week back log of cases and won't get to yours prior to that three weeks, or they may know that the MC doctor has only a three day lag in case reviews. In this case, if the DE says it will take the psych MC three weeks to get to your case, then you should not call prior to that time as you will be spinning your wheels as well as wasting the DEs time.

While you can help the claims DE write up your case faster through your status check calls, you cannot get him/her to force a psychologist or medical doctor to review or skip over other cases ahead of yours without a really good reason.

The list of really good reasons include: if your doctor tells you that you only have six months to live (i.e. your condition is terminal) or if you have been placed in an assisted living home or you can no longer walk without a medically prescribed cane or walker or you are now on kidney dialysis due to chronic renal failure. All these cases generally result in your claim being allowed, and cases that are allowances are written up before cases that are going to be denials).

The bright side of this is that, generally, after the examiner writes up a medical summary of the claim, if s/he strongly feels that your case will result in an approval, s/he can issue something called a "presumptive disability" (PD) decision at that time which will allow you to receive benefits while you await the final decision. But this is only true if you have an SSI claim or if you have a combination claim that includes eligibility for Supplemental Security Income.

Action Step 3: If you have applied for disability, find a calendar and use it to jot down the dates that you will be calling your examiner for status updates. The dates can fluctuate from the schedule I have outlined here, but it is important that you call periodically if you want a quicker decision on your claim.

STEP 4:
DETERMINE IF YOU CAN BE GRANTED TEMPORARY BENEFITS WHILE YOUR CLAIM IS BEING PROCESSED

Sometimes claimants who are severely disabled can be granted disability payments "presumptively" under the Presumptive Disability (PD) program. This means that you can receive benefits for up to six months while your claim is being processed.

According to Social Security disability law, if you are applying for SSI or a combination of SSDI and SSI, and the claims examiner has reason to believe strongly that your claim will be an approval, then he can grant you presumptive disability benefits immediately.

Who Determines If You Qualify for Expedited Presumptive Disability Payments?

While SSA regulations allow the decision to be made in the Field Office of SSA, or by a claims examiner in the state contracting DDS or DAS offices, it has been my experience in the two states that I served in that the Field Office, the office that accepts your initial application, **never** makes this decision on a claim.

That is unfortunate because it would mean faster benefits to those with obviously disabling impairments.

What Conditions Qualify You for Getting Expedited PD Payments?

There are some medical conditions listed in the SSA "Blue Book" that might qualify you for PD benefits. Most metastatic cancers are among them; chronic renal failure with dialysis is another that comes to mind. However, listing those conditions that might qualify you for expedited payments while a decision is made on your claim is beyond the scope of this guide. The intent is just to make you aware of the existence of the program.

Examiners have a lot of flexibility in deciding whom they grant PD benefits to. And although it is an area that shows up on internal employee evaluation forms, many examiners do not do a good job in scanning a claimant's initial application to determine if expedited benefits are warranted. You may be able to help them remember the existence of the PD program just by asking them: *"Do you think I might qualify for expedited PD benefits?"*

The good news though is that if you are granted PD, it means the likelihood that you will be granted benefits is great since examiners are not allowed to grant these benefits to claimants that they do not feel will eventually qualify for benefits once all the medical/vocation evidence is received.

The other good part about receiving expedited benefits is that if you are granted these presumptive payments for up to six months, it comes with medical benefits (Medicaid) as well, and if you are subsequently denied benefits on your claim—for whatever reason—you do not have to repay any monies received under the program.

As an aside, I once granted Presumptive Disability benefits to a claimant who had cancer. He did not meet the blue book listing but I granted PD benefits anyway. The claimant needed to have treatments that he would not be able to get without medical insurance. I felt that though his condition did not currently meet the requirement for disability benefits, that if he did not receive PD benefits with the Medicaid attached, then his claim would ultimately come back and be an allowance, but only after his cancer had progressed.

So I granted him PD benefits, held off on deciding his claim for as long as I could and then had to deny his claim because his condition did not meet SSA's definition for disability. My reasoning was that if the claimant did not have Medicaid and did not get medical treatment, he would be back in later with a condition more severe and then be granted benefits, plus he would return "more" sicker and in worst condition, perhaps even with metastatic cancer when he returned.

While it is true that I may have bent the rules a little to get this claimant benefits—something I rarely did--I felt it was my duty as a thinking human being to handle the claim that way. Why let an individual's condition deteriorate on a technicality before granting benefits that could save the claimant much agony in the short term, and the government more money in the long run.

Action Step 4: You should ask your examiner if you might qualify for the Presumptive Disability program.

STEP 5:
PRESENTING YOUR VOCATIONAL HISTORY AND YOUR MEDICAL RECORDS

In step two, it was asked that you complete your disability application with a focus on function. This means that you should include information that is very telling about what you can and cannot still do as a result of your impairments.

Vocational Assessment

The language used when you present such information should be written in statements that tell of your ability (or inability) to perform basic work functions. Below are terms used to assess certain physical and mental abilities, which might be required in the workplace. So these are terms you want to use in explaining what you had to do to function at your last job, if you had one.

Work functions, including physical abilities to:

- Lift
- Carry
- Stand
- Walk
- Sit
- Push
- Pull
- Climb

- Balance
- Stoop
- Kneel
- Crouch
- Crawl
- Reach
- Handle
- Finger
- Feel
- See
- Hear
- Speak

In certain jobs, you might be exposed to certain environmental conditions, such as:

- Heat
- Cold
- Wetness
- Noise
- Vibration
- Hazards
- Humidity

If any of your jobs required exposure to these things, please list them on your work history form, especially if your current medical condition would prevent you from returning to work that required one or more of those exposures.

Mental Functions, including the ability or limited ability to:

- Remember location, work-like procedures
- Carry out instructions
- Perform activities within a schedule
- Be punctual
- Sustain ordinary routine without special supervision
- Work in coordination/proximity to others
- Accept instructions/respond appropriately to criticism
- Maintain socially appropriate behavior
- Set realistic goals

- Be aware of normal hazards/take precautions
- Travel in unfamiliar places/use public transportation
- Adhere to basic standards of neatness/cleanliness
- Understand, remember instructions
- Maintain attention/concentration
- Make independent plans
- Make work-related decisions
- Interact appropriately with others
- Ask questions/request assistance
- Respond appropriately to changes

Accurately Describing Your Functional Limitations

So, for example, a descriptive statement that you might write on your application alleging a physical impairment might read:

> *"For the past 15 years I have worked as a painter which required me to be able to **stand** 6 to 8 hours a day, **climb** ladders, **lift** 10-15 pounds constantly, and move **heavy** furniture occasionally which could weigh up to 100 lbs. or more. Since falling off the ladder 9 months ago and my subsequent back surgeries, I have not been able to return to painting or to lift anything over 10 lbs., per my doctor's instructions. My recurring inner ear disease doesn't help either because I can no longer safely **climb** a ladder."*

[Note: the above is the sample description referred to in Action Step #2)

If a claimant includes such a statement on the application, and it proves to be "credible" based on the medical evidence later gathered in file, then it indicates that without a doubt, this applicant cannot return to his previous occupation.

Now, I have to say that not much weight is ever given to claimant's statements if they are not backed up by objective medical evidence. The same holds true for such statements from a treating physician if it is not backed up by objective evidence found in the medical records. Still, what this claimant's statement would do for the examiner when he/she reviews your application for the first time is that it would clue him in to the exact functional limitations you would be facing if you tried to return to your old job.

And, depending on the education and age of the individual, the examiner would be able to determine immediately the kind of objective tests or results he would need to see in the medical records to be able to approve the claim. (For more details, see article _The First 15 Minutes_ sited on the online resource page at back of Plan).

In cases alleging a physical disability, such statements of function from both the claimant and / or a treating physician must be determined to be "credible", "not credible" or "partially credible" on the Residual Functioning Form. This form is completed on all cases alleging a physical disability.

For mental allegations, examiners use the Mental Residual Functioning form to assess the extent of mental limitations. This form is used in conjunction with a Psychiatric Review Technique Form if your psychological condition is deemed to be severe.

So let's move on to your medical records.

Medical Records … The Heart of your Claim

There must be medical records in your claim file in order to determine if you are eligible for disability based on your condition. Those medical records are used to gleam the objective or subjective evidence that supports your disability claim.

When your claim is received by the examiner in the DDS office, one of the first things he will do is send a letter to all your medical providers requesting a copy of your medical file.

The physicians, medical specialist, psychologists, counselors, hospitals – whoever you have indicated has your records – are asked to return the information as soon as possible to the claims worker. The letters are computerized and sent out by the examiner the very day when your claim reaches the claims examiner's hands.

If the examiner is not able to locate your medical providers based on the information on your application, and is unable to find an address for them in the database, you might receive a phone call asking for clarification.

When there are Problems Getting Your Medical Records

Most of your medical providers will send your medical records out as requested without incident. Some, however, will send an automated notice back telling the claims examiner what their policy is regarding mailing medical records, and this usually means they are requesting payment up front for those records.

Such a notice slows your claim down considerably.

Number one, because the DDS claims examiner and the DDS offices have few provisions to pay for medical records, and the ones that they do have means the examiner must forward the request to another department. Whenever you have to send something to another department in a bureaucracy, get ready for delays and problems.

Ultimately, from an examiner's perspective, this means that the records that this particular medical facility has on you might never be received or evaluated by your claims examiner. If it is your primary treating physician who has the majority of your medical records, then this could put you at a real disadvantage in getting your claim allowed. Keep in mind that without medical evidence to support your claim, you have no claim.

But bottom-line, examiners have no incentive to try to get these records for you because it just takes too much time. Anything that is out of the norm in claims processing takes additional time, and thus it is much easier for the examiner to just set the claimant up for a consultative medical exam (CE) rather than try to get the state to pay for medical records from your treating physician.

At this point, some examiners will place a courtesy call to the claimant to request assistance in getting the medical facility to release the records to try to speed the process up. This would be true only if the claim is a regular SS Disability Insurance claim, and is not a mental allegation case. Examiners are trained not to request assistance from claimants who are SSI applicants. Do not ask me why this is so. Medical records coming from a regular treating physician are always preferred over the results of a one-time consultative exam by a non-treating physician. So any assistance that any claimant or their representative can give in getting TP records should be vigorously pursued.

If Your Physician is Supportive of Your Disability Claim

If your regular treating physician supports your claim for disability, i.e. agrees with you that you are disabled and unable to work, this can be an ace in the hole, but only if your doctor knows how to word his letter of support to the DDS claims office. The more s/he uses the language of function in his letter and connects it to the objective medical evidence in your medical file, the more useful the letter will be.

You can ask your doctor to write a letter to the DDS office in support of your claim. But do remember that a letter that says "I believe (claimant) is totally disabled and should be granted disability benefits," is worthless. You might as well have signed the letter yourself. Examiners get these type generic letters all the time.

On the other hand, if your doctor takes the extra step and writes it as though he is speaking directly to another medical doctor or psychologist, such as the one who will be reviewing your claim, and he states why he believes you are disabled and mentions the objective evidence to support his position, then you have a shot for the letter to do some good.

It cannot be stressed too much that the opinions of your treating doctors—when they are backed with reference to the objective or even subjective evidence—will always be given more weight than the opinion of any consultative doctor who has only seen you once, as is the case when Social Security sends you to one of their physicians or psychologists for a consultative examination.

For example, the letter from your doctor in a physical disability claim might read much like the one on the next page.

Sample Function Letter from Your Treating Physician (Dr.'s Letterhead)

To Whom It May Concern:

I have treated John Q Public for 10 years and am fully aware of his physical limitations and medical condition.

I believe he is disabled from sustaining any type of work due to his spinal misalignment occurring at disk __ and disk___ (see x-rays dated 9/29/2009 in his medical records).

Mr. Public currently comes in for back injections __ times per month because the pain is so great.

Due to this condition, his range of motion in his back is _____, as of his exam-dated _8/30/09__. Because of this, he is unable to lift more than 5 lbs. occasionally.

Mr. Public also suffers from advanced cardiovascular disease that has left him with an ejection fraction of ____ (see test dated 9/15/2009 in medical records). This means Mr. Public cannot walk the 25 feet to his mailbox without stopping for a rest.

Mr. Public currently uses a motorized wheel chair for ambulation at home and in public because of these impairments, and in my opinion, it would be impossible for Mr. Public to stand to do his previous job as a carpenter, and he would not be able to sit more than 2 hours at a time to do even light or sedentary type work because of his constant need to change positions to keep the pain in his back at bay.

Please let me know if I can provide any additional information or further clarification to help you reach the same conclusion that I have, and that is that Mr. Public is permanently and totally disabled from working any job.

Sincerely, Benjamin T. DeCarte, MD

.

Now, wouldn't it be great if your doctor knew exactly what medical information the disability examiner was looking for before he wrote such a letter?

He can. A copy of the SS Blue Book *"Disability Evaluation under Social Security"* September 2008 edition is available online. It reads:

Disability Evaluation under Social Security
(Blue Book- September 2008)

This edition of Disability Evaluation under Social Security, (also known as the Blue Book), has been specially prepared to provide physicians and other health professionals with an understanding of the disability programs administered by the Social Security Administration. It explains how each program works, and the kinds of information a health professional can furnish to help ensure sound and prompt decisions on disability claims.

The Adult and Childhood Listings of Impairments are included in this publication. These listings are just part of how we decide if someone is disabled. We also consider past work experience, severity of medical conditions, age, education, and work skills.

This electronic version replaces the June 2006 and prior editions of Disability Evaluation under Social Security.

SSA Pub. No. 64-039
ICN 468600
September 2008

This Book is generally updated every few years by the SSA.

This guide is the exact same one used by your examiner. Still, in adjudicating claims, it may be true that your doctor might not have time to review all sections of the blue book, but he could look up the section pertaining to your condition and note what SSA requires as proof of a disabling condition.

If you have a representative or are a representative for someone applying for benefits, your time would be well spent finding the few pages or paragraphs in the blue book that pertain to your client's specific disability, and then forwarding a copy of the pages to the treating physician with your request for a letter of support. Going one step further, you could also draft the letter for the physician to review and sign.

For example, if the claimant is alleging back problems, i.e. a disorder involving the spine, you could go to the blue book, figure out that this would be a muscular skeletal condition, go to that section and print out the section there that reads:

> **1.04 *Disorders of the spine*** (e.g., herniated nucleus pulposus, spinal arachnoiditis, spinal stenosis, osteoarthritis, degenerative disc disease, facet arthritis, vertebral fracture), resulting in compromise of a nerve root (including the cauda equina) or the spinal cord. ***With** (my emphasis)*:
>
> A. Evidence of nerve root compression characterized by neuro-anatomic distribution of pain, limitation of motion of the spine, motor loss (atrophy with associated muscle weakness or muscle weakness) accompanied by sensory or reflex loss and, if there is involvement of the lower back, positive straight-leg raising test (sitting and supine);
>
> OR
>
> B. Spinal arachnoiditis, confirmed by an operative note or pathology report of tissue biopsy, or by appropriate medically acceptable imaging, manifested by severe burning or painful dysesthesia, resulting in the need for changes in position or posture more than once every 2 hours;
>
> OR
>
> C. Lumbar spinal stenosis resulting in pseudoclaudication, established by findings on appropriate medically acceptable imaging, manifested by chronic nonradicular pain and weakness, and resulting in inability to ambulate effectively, as defined in 1.00B2b.

In this example, you will note first of all a lot of medical terms that you might not have a clue as to the meaning. However, what you can decipher is that specific conditions will require specific requirements as to what SSA will accept as being proof positive of a severely disabling condition worthy of a claims allowance.

You can see from the example that not only must the condition exist, but it has to exist **with** either a or b or c attached as prerequisites for a guaranteed claims approval.

And that is where the physician would be able to say definitely in his letter of support if the claimant had any one of those prerequisites attached to his diagnoses and disability.

As mentioned before, another thing about a letter from your treating physician stating that you are disabled, with the pertinent facts and evidence to explain his logic, is that his word will carry much more weight than SSA medical doctors who see you once and give an opinion. And this is a good thing in your favor.

I can remember a couple of cases where all I needed was a letter from a claimant's treating physician (TP) saying that the applicant has to use an assistive device for ambulation/mobility. While this may seem minor to you because you are using the device daily, keep in mind that if there is no documentation anywhere in the medical records that you use a wheelchair for ambulation, then you cannot assume your claims examiner who never sees you or the medical consultant who never sees you will just know this. Sometimes this fact just slips out as you are talking to the claimant about other case matters. The examiner then says, "Gee I wish you had said that from the beginning." Sometimes in these cases, examiners are able to fax the doctor a letter with a statement saying, "Patient has used a wheelchair for ambulation since _____(date/year), etc." Then all the doctor has to do is sign it.

Again, this goes back to the focus on function. Please. Please. Please keep in mind that the disability examiner and medical consultant will never see you in person so all they know is what you tell them and what's in your medical record. Whenever I used to get well-crafted supporting letters from TPs who were making a case for giving their patients disability, I used to silently thank them for making my job so much easier.

Consultative Examinations: What It Means When You are Asked to Attend One

Let's talk about consultative examinations for a moment since many claimants are referred to see an outside doctor, as it is helpful to know what is happening and what to expect.

If you are asked to attend a consultative examination (CE), it means one thing and one thing only: there is not enough objective or subjective evidence in your medical record file to make a decision on your claim based on the policies and regulations that SSA mandates. The information in your medical records might be outdated or non-existent, or it might not be to the exact specifications that SSA requires for your particular condition / allegation.

A good example would be that of a claimant alleging a respiratory condition such as COPD, Chronic Obstructive Pulmonary Disease. Once the examiner sees the diagnosis, they will look in the medical records for FEV values. What are FEV values? The claims examiner has no idea since he is not a medical doctor, but he does know that according to SSA's "Blue Book", which he consults, he knows that the claimant must have an FEV value equal to or less than the values outlined in the chart to qualify for disability based on that particular condition.

If there are no FEV values in the claimant's medical records, the examiner must obtain these values, either by asking the claimant to go to his regular physician to have the specific test performed or by scheduling a Consultative Examination to have the test performed.

Generally, the examiner opts for a CE because it is more "routine" than asking a claimant to ask his regular doctor to do it. Why? Some reasons are that the claimant may no longer have medical insurance due to his disability or due to being out of work and unable to pay for it, or a host of other reasons, all of which are avoided if the examiner just schedules a consultative exam with one of SSA's contracting medical physicians. Plus, the CE doctor knows the exact testing SSA needs because it is spelled out in the referral notice, so when the results come in, it is assured that it will be the information needed to make a decision on the claim.

But, many claimants think they are being shafted when they are asked to attend a CE because they reason that they already have a regular treating physician and why do they need to see an outside doctor. They think SSA is setting them up for a claim denial because doctors that contract with SSA are on the "payroll" and might not provide an accurate or impartial assessment.

By this point, many claimants are outraged because they are wondering why the consultative exam has been set up when their doctors have all of their records. In their moment of "madness", they decide not to keep the appointment, thinking it will force the examiner to use the medical records in file. What they do not realize is that the treating physician (TP) may be withholding the records, for whatever reason.

But, another reason it is not a good strategy to fail to keep a CE appointment is because your claim can be denied simply because you fail to keep the appointment, so you lose either way in this situation if you do not keep your appointment.

Social Security rules require that certain assessments and tests be in file for certain conditions, and that medical information must be current. If the needed records are not in file, and your TP will not provide them, the CE must be scheduled if there is any chance of you receiving an allowance on your claim. Remember we said: No medical records=no allowance of disability benefits.

When claimants treat Consultative Exam appointments lightly, it frustrates claims examiners to no end. If you are looking to get on the wrong side of your examiner, go ahead and miss your CE appointment. Call to say you cannot make a CE appointment because of (you insert reason) or because (insert another reason). If there has not been a death in your immediate family and your medical condition permits, try to keep your first CE appointment. This will make your claims examiner very happy.

Why? It is because examiners are evaluated on the timeliness of their claims decisions. If you add 30-75 days to their processing time for a missed CE appointment, his or her attitude towards you may take a dive. The logic is: if this person is truly disabled and truly in need of assistance, then why is this exam not important to them? Why is this exam not a priority for them?" While I am not defending this attitude among examiners, I am trying to give you information to help you assist yourself and your worker in decreasing the amount of time it will take for you to get a decision on your claim.

Clues on Your Application that Tell the Examiner a Consultative Exam (CE) Might Be Needed

Some consultative exams are scheduled by claims examiner the minute they receive your claim application. This might be the case if you indicate you have:

a) No treating physician and you have not been to the doctor in the past three months
b) You have a treating physician but your last visit was more than three months ago and you do not indicate an upcoming visit in the next few weeks
c) You indicate a psychological impairment but have no mental health providers listed on your medical contact list
d) You list mental retardation, but there are no sources listed that could provide needed IQ scores

These situations inform the examiner that even if some medical records come in, that they will still need to be supplemented with current medical records. Since the disability assessment is based on your current level of functioning, records must be current.

About Your Consultative Exam (CE) and What to Do If You Feel the Physician or Psychologist Is Not Competent

Medical and psychological consultative examinations (CE) are provided by licensed doctors, medical specialists and/or psychologists who contract with Social Security to provide the information needed by the DDS office to make a decision on a claim.

You will not be sent to a chiropractor to assess your back injuries because their specialty is not one which is on the list of medical providers the SSA deems appropriate to assess such conditions. There are various criteria and credentials that consultative medical examiners must meet in order to qualify to contract with the SSA to be a service provider.

Still, if you feel that your CE doctor mistreated you in any way or was not competent to assess your medical condition, you can report that to the DDS office. A special unit handles such complaints against CE doctors. They will investigate and make a finding, and if warranted (as in the case of a CE doctor receiving many complaints), their contract with SSA could be terminated.

Special Medical Conditions...Allegations of Pain, CFS and Fibromyalgia

In many ways, as a claims examiner, I much preferred having to adjudicate a claim where the claimant was only alleging a physical disability because the objective evidence was so much more readily available or could be easily obtained to prove or disapprove the allegation.

Many people allege back problems in disability claims, this condition probably running neck and neck with the number of people alleging high blood pressure, diabetes and high cholesterol. Still, back problems were easy to adjudicate because you could get x-rays and "range of motion" studies, and in rare cases even functional reports to demonstrate the extent of the limitations the impairment placed on a claimant's ability to move or function in a given work environment.

Allegation of pain, on the other hand, proved to be a much more subjective area, and consequently these claims are more difficult to adjudicate. Examiners do not handle cases involving disabling pain very well because the Social Security Administration does not train them well in this area.

This is why I suggest that if you have an issue with serious, disabling pain as an element of your disability, that you consider seeking legal representation or a disability advocate or representative to help you present your case to an Administrative Law Judge after you are denied benefits at the initial level and / or reconsideration level.

Persons with chronic fatigue syndrome or fibromyalgia were routinely given "medium level" work exertional levels in both states that I served in. What that meant from a practical perspective was that these claims were routinely denied because if you can do medium level work, you will not be found to be disabled, unless accompanied by a severe mental impairment or another disabling condition. There would be too many medium, light and sedentary exertional level jobs in the marketplace that you might be capable of doing.

So, persons with these conditions can generally expect a long battle in their quest to get disability benefits.

Vocational / Work History

We discussed work functions previously, but we come back to it because ultimately in SS disability claims, the final decision is whether you can return to your past work, not return to your past work or can do any other type work.

Your vocational functional assessment is literally the last determination that is made on your claim before a decision is made, but it can sometimes make a difference between getting benefits or not.

While it is true that you cannot change which jobs you did in the last 15 years, you can influence how the claims examiner "sees" your job by clearly describing what it was that you did in an 8-hour work day.

On the one hand, disability examiners will refer to the Dictionary of Occupational Titles (DOT) to see what people in your job position typically do in an 8-hour workday, still, this might not be what you did in your typical 8-hour shift.

For example, you might have had a dual job title, with one position requiring only sedentary, supervisory type deskwork while the second required training new employees to learn to do medium level work.

One job required lifting only files and office papers, while the second required showing new employees how to use a forklift and to move 50-100 pound pallets in a warehouse environment.

Unless you spell it out, the examiner will go with the definitions found in the DOT manual. And that might or might not account for what you actually had to do on your job.

By completing each work history question thoroughly on the work history form, you paint the picture of precisely what physical requirements were needed on your job. Examiners will generally go with your description of what you did on your job versus the DOT data, unless there is some compelling reason not to.

Once I received a claim that could have been a "reconsideration" case, but it came to me as a new case, perhaps because the claimant filed outside of her 60 day time period for a reconsideration. Anyway, I got the case. The claimant was a 55-year-old woman who had been a hotel room cleaner for many years. She had listed on her work history form that she lifted 10-15 lbs. on a daily basis. And, the previous examiner had accepted her word for what she lifted at face value; however, I did not. So I called the claimant, knowing that these type workers generally are classified as "medium level" exertional workers (i.e. have to lift up to 50 lbs. occasionally in a workday). And I asked her to tell me what she specifically did in her job on a daily basis, and, just as I suspected, the actual work of pushing and pulling vacuum cleaners, sometimes moving beds or dressers back in place meant that she routinely actually lifted more than 15 pounds in a day.

Then, based on her medical records already in file, which had evidence that she could no longer do "medium" level work, and given her advanced age, was able to allow her claim without one more piece of evidence except her statement of her daily work activities.

What I did was not extraordinary, but it does demonstrate that it is all in the detail. You absolutely must paint as thorough a picture of your daily work activities on the work history form because not every examiner will make that phone call. There might not be time in their day to do it. This individual's claim could easily have been another denial, especially since her medical evidence would have all remained the same.

The other reason I mention this story is because most experienced examiners know of the four or five different occupations that carry a "medium level" work exertional level even though the DOT might list them as "light level" workers. If an inexperienced examiner had gotten this case for review, it could have slipped through the cracks.

Truck drivers often fall into the same situation. They think that just because they make a delivery and are not required to move any of the cargo, that their jobs are considered light work. This is not true. Again, experienced adjudicators know that it is more than likely that with all the climbing into the cab, and pulling and getting in and out of the truck, and working with the big steering wheel and clutches, that truck drivers can be considered medium level workers.

So I cannot stress enough that an accurate description of what you did on your job can literally change a decision from a denial to an approval, especially in cases of older or advanced aged individuals.

Action Step 5: When you are completing the work history form, do not gloss over the items that ask how long you stood, stooped, climbed, etc. Accurately detailing what you did and how long you were required to do it on your job is especially important if you are over 50, 55, 60.

If you have a mental disability, noting the physical requirements of your job are not nearly as important as noting the mental ones. For example, if you were a supervisor who suffered a head injury that affected your ability to remember detailed instructions, you (or your representative) would want to list that fact somewhere on your application. It would indicate you might no longer be capable of skilled level work, but could now only do unskilled work.

So whatever your disability, thoroughly answer all questions related to your work history for the last 15 years. The examiner will be able to find most of your jobs in the Dictionary of Occupational Titles and the resulting exertional level and skill level, but if you did things that were not typical for that position, you should be sure to highlight those additional work functions.

It is understood that the examiner is trying to determine if you can return to any of your old jobs, so be clear about what those old jobs really required you to do, functionally.

As with every area of your application, if you have already completed the work history form, but realize you did not do a thorough job in its completion, you can always send in an addendum or statement telling the examiner in detail what you did on your job(s).

STEP 6:
HOW TO DETERMINE IF YOU HAVE A SEVERE IMPAIRMENT OR A REALISTIC CHANCE OF RECEIVING BENEFITS

The Social Security Administration uses terms like "severe" or "non-severe" or "more than non-severe" to categorize impairments. If your medical condition is considered "non-severe", it means that it will not affect your ability to work, or influence it only minimally, and you will be denied benefits at Step 2 of the Five Step Sequential Evaluation process.

So how do examiners determine if your impairments are severe?

Some impairments are obviously severe, but if yours is borderline, how will you know?

Well, let me start by saying that many claimants have high blood pressure (HBP), high cholesterol, diabetes and back pain. And, millions of people are on antidepressant drugs or anti-anxiety drugs.

We'll start with HBP. You have it. You are on medication. It is controlled with medication. This condition will result in a "denial" of benefits. It is considered non-severe because it is a condition that is being controlled with medication.

Ok, maybe your HBP is not completely controlled with your meds. SSA says that unless this condition has resulted in you experiencing end organ damage (EOD) because of it, then it is not disabling in and of itself. EOD means that your HBP is so out of control that it has led to other organs being damaged and affected by it, organs within the circulatory system such as your heart, eyes, kidneys or brain.

Now, let's take diabetes. The statistics on who has this disease in America are staggering. Millions of people have it. Social Security Disability would go belly up bankrupt if every person who had it got benefits. Like HBP, your diabetes must be out of control and you must have other chronic symptoms before it moves into the realm of being considered a severe impairment by the SSA.

But, what if you break an arm, a leg and cannot do your normal work for months while the limb heals? Your claim is denied; not because you can do your regular work, but because this is a condition that is "expected to resolve to non-severe" in less than a year. If you have a medical condition now that you will probably not have within a year, then your claim will be denied.

If however, you broke your ankle -- which is considered a weight bearing joint -- and during the healing it never united back properly, you then may be diagnosed with a "non-union" fracture, in which case, disability may be established if all other criteria are met.

We already mentioned how SSA looks at (or used to look at) claims alleging Fibromyalgia and CFS. These are generally claim denials at the initial and reconsideration level. Other conditions that often prove to be denials are:

- Hepatitis B & C

- Seizures that are somewhat controlled with medications

- Vision in only one eye or hearing in only one ear.

These conditions will all yield claim denials, so there is no need to get your hopes up.

Psychological illnesses where your medical prescription dose is the same as everyone else in America will be denials. You will not receive benefits if you are mildly depressed or anxious. We all are at times. Remember, your ailment has to severely affect your ability to work a regular full time job without too much disturbance.

My first case when i worked with legal aide as a disability paralegal involved a young woman in her early 20s who filed for disability alleging asthma. Now, getting disability for asthma is easy if you meet certain specific requirements regarding hospital visits, etc., as outlined in the <u>*SSA blue book*</u>*. But her symptoms and manifestations of the disease did not meet the criteria and she had been denied a couple of times. Well, her medical records showed some psychological issues as well, especially when we started to explore the fact that she could not hold a job. It was her inability to work around others, her inability to speak appropriately to others, etc., that ultimately allowed her to receive disability benefits.*

Many people with psychological problems are not aware of the extent of their mental challenges, but it is the combination of those mental problems when assessed in light of physical impairments that can result in a claims allowance.

Action Step 6: If you have a regular treating physician, ask him or her if your condition would prevent you from doing any type of full time work for at least one year. If s/he says yes, then your condition might be considered severe by SSA adjudicators.

STEP 7:

SHOULD YOU TRY TO WORK WHILE AWAITING A DECISION ON YOUR CLAIM?

Many claimants ask this question while they await a decision on their claim. And the official answer goes something like this: "If you think you can work, go ahead and give it a try."

Many times claimants ask this question because bills are due and they feel they must do something to keep the bear at bay.

SSA has many provisions for allowing someone to attempt to work while disabled. You can have a trial work period that will not be counted against you.

Having said that, I want to also say this: Claims examiners in DDS offices are not thoroughly trained on all the provisions of "trial work" periods, so what generally happens is that once you report that you have gone back to work—to make ends meet—and your income is over the allowable limit, the examiner simply sends your claim back to the Field Office for review. What happens after that, I do not know. But, logically speaking, if your claim is no longer in the office that determines medical disability, how will you ever be approved for disability benefits?

In other words, the disability fact-finding review of your case ceases. The other subtle message you send when you go on a trial work period during your disability application is that you are able to do some type of work, especially if you do the new job full time. If you can sustain an eight-hour workday schedule, then how can you at the same time be unable to work?

Once you are getting disability benefits, you might participate in a trial work period (TWP) for up to 9 months at which time SSA will evaluate your status to determine if you are engaging in SGA. If they determine that you are, then you can receive an additional three months of benefits before your case is terminated.

So the rules are a bit different for the person who is already receiving benefits versus those who are still being evaluated for disability.

Action Step 7: The rules and regulations governing TWPs are complex so you may need to contact SSA to get clarification on any questions you might have.

STEP 8:
RECEIVING, READING AND INTERPRETING YOUR "NOTICE OF DECISION" LETTER

Once your claim is decided and the examiner inputs the decision into the computerized system, a letter is generated which is printed out and placed in your file to be mailed out once the Field Office receives the file. (Note: This process has no doubt changed now that SSA has gone to a "paperless" file). The letter looks like it is sent from the national SSA office, but it is generated in the DDS office and prepared there for mailing.

But the letter cannot actually be mailed by the DDS at this time because your claim may be randomly chosen for review by the DDS quality review team before it is returned to the Field Office for final processing.

A quality reviewer has the power to remand the case back to the examiner with instructions for follow-up actions. This can happen if the reviewer does not believe the examiner made a good decision based on the MER in file, or did not follow proper procedure and policy, or if he believes additional information is needed prior to the issuance of a decision.

This is where things like "is the medical evidence on file recent enough or is it more than xxx days old" will come into play. Or, is the date that the claimant alleged disability and the date that the examiner established disability consistent, and if not, has the examiner noted the difference and explained why in the "Notice of Decision" letter. If retroactive benefits are allowed, does the medical evidence support disability on the date decided on by the examiner?

In essence, it is the quality reviewers' job to ensure that all kinds of legal and technical case requirements ensuring the integrity of the decision based on SSAs rules and regulations have been followed.

I'm explaining this process not because you need to know it, but to tell you that it will do you no good to ask your claims examiner what decision was made on your claim because they may not know. They know the decision they entered, but if your claim is selected for review, they know that that decision has the potential to be changed, and consequently they are not allowed to tell you over the phone what their decision was.

Reading Your "Notice of Decision" Letter for Clues on How to Best Proceed

So your *Notice of Decision* letter has finally arrived. It looks differently from the other letters you have received from the SSA. This one appears to be from the National Office of the SSA, and so you open it reluctantly, but still with a bit of anticipation.

There are only three scenarios that will be presented in the letter:

- You have been allowed benefits, and the date of your allowance is the same date that you said your disability began.

- You have been allowed benefits and the date of your allowance is a date different from the date you said your disability began.

- You have been denied benefits and there is a brochure attached explaining to you how to file for reconsideration or an appeal of the decision.

Let's take a more detailed look at claims approval and denials and what it means.

Your Claim is Approved

SSDI

If you are approved for benefits, and you have applied for Social Security Disability either alone or in combination with SSI benefits, you should be sure to note the date that benefits were allowed.

If this date is the same as your alleged disability date, then there is nothing else to do except await the next step in the process.

If the date is not the same as your alleged disability date, there should be some explanation in the letter as to why a different date was established as the onset of disability. If you disagree with the determination of your disability start date, then you should follow the instructions in the letter that explain how you can dispute it.

SSI

If you are an SSI applicant and your claim has been approved, generally there is no leeway for arguing a prior date. SSI benefits can begin the month of application with no provision for back benefits, even if you allege a different disability start date.

Still, if you have been waiting on your decision on your claim for any period of time, say six months, one year or more, you should qualify for retroactive benefits back to the month of application. That is why it is extremely important that you file for a re-consideration if your claim is initially denied because if you subsequently win your claim, your retroactive benefits will go back to the original initial application date if you were disabled on that date.

If on the other hand, you merely file a new application if you are denied benefits, then you forfeit the right to have benefits before that new application date, and that can literally mean you have given away thousands of dollars that could have been yours if you had filed for a reconsideration rather than just filed a new application.

There is a provision for retroactive Medicaid benefits in SSI claims, so your examiner can grant retroactive Medicaid for 30-90 days prior to your application date. This is especially helpful if you incurred a lot of unpaid hospital bills and medical bills prior to the date of your disability benefits allowance.

So, even if you have been approved for benefits, be sure to check the date you have been approved for, i.e. when SSA says your disability began, especially if you have an SSDI claim. Unlike SSI claims, you might be entitled to benefits prior to your date of application if it can be proven that your disability started prior to that date.

Your Claim is Denied

The Reasons

If your claim is denied, there should be some indication in the letter stating why. Some states are more thorough than others in providing a specific explanation as to the reason for denial. Others just indicate in broad terms whether SSA believes you are not disabled because you can return to your past work, to other work, or that your condition was determined to be non-severe, or that it is expected to resolve itself within a year.

Another reason for denial may be that you failed to keep two consultative exam (CE) appointments and thus the evidence of your disability could not be substantiated. If you fail to keep two CE appointments, this is viewed as non-cooperation and is grounds for a denial in physical disability cases. In mental claims, there is a little more leniency in missing CE appointments, but the examiner will try to close cases where claimants are not cooperating at the earliest possible time. This is why you need to try to find someone who can assist you in remembering or attending a CE appointment if you have a mental disability.

Important Things to Look For In Your "Notice of Decision" Letter

There are clues in your denial letter that can give you an indication of whether you have a fighting chance at receiving benefits or whether your chances are slim to nil that you will ever receive benefits.

Can Do "Past Work" Versus Can Do "Other Work" Decisions

Regardless of the reason given for your denial, what you are looking for in the denial notice is whether it stated that you could return to your past work based on the medical / vocational evidence in file, or whether it asserts that you can do other work based on the evidence in file.

If the denial says you can do your past work, then it indicates you will have a more difficult time in your appeal or reconsideration application than if it says that you can no longer do your past work but should be able to do other work.

The latter indicates that your condition is definitely a severe one, especially since it has affected you to the point that you cannot return to your past line of work. That means you have jumped over more than one hurdle toward being granted benefits and it may just be a matter of now proving that there is no other work that you would be able to do in the national economy based on your impairments, your age, skill level and education.

So a letter that says you cannot do your past work but can do other work is definitely more positive for you than one that says you can go back to your old job.

In terms of a reconsideration of such a decision on your claim, should you choose to file, it will begin under the assumption that you cannot do your past job.

If you are 54 and a half when you get that decision, it means you would be well advised to reapply for benefits when your age bracket changes. Once you are determined to be of advanced age or approaching retirement, the vocational rules change so that if you can no longer do your past job, then it may not be anticipated that you will be able to adjust to a new line of work.

"Expected to Resolve to Non-Severe" Denials

If your "Notice of Decision" letter indicates that "although you are currently disabled, your medical condition is expected to resolve to non-severe within the year", there is generally very little remedy for this one. One example where you might have a fighting chance is if your condition has already lasted for a year—while you awaited disability benefits—and it is still disabling. As mentioned prior, this may be the case where there is a fracture of a weight bearing joint, and it has not healed correctly or the reunion of the bone did not occur as your doctor(s) anticipated.

Condition is "Non-Severe" Denials

Finally, if your decision states that you were denied because your condition is non-severe, it means you will have a tough row to tow in getting an approval on your claim. If you will recall the five step sequential evaluation process, having a severe impairment is step 2 of the process, so if your impairment is not deemed to be severe, your likelihood of winning at any of the subsequent reconsideration and appeal levels are not that great.

Again, conditions such as controlled HBP and high cholesterol or mild depression would generally fall into this category.

The "Just Keep Applying" Myth of Getting Disability

Everyone knows that most people who apply for disability benefits are denied the first time around. Statistics can give you the exact ratios.

Many people feel that all they have to do is just keep reapplying and they will eventually be approved.

But, is the reason that you got disability the fourth or fifth time around because of your persistence, or because your condition actually deteriorated during that time and got worst?

Or, might it have been that your condition / impairment is still the same, but your age bracket has changed, i.e. you progressed from a "younger individual" to one of "advanced age?"

SSA "vocational" disability rules are different for persons in different age groups, especially as it relates to physical disabilities.

Just something to consider.

KNOWLEDGE IS POWER...

I can remember my mom had suffered a few heart attacks when she first applied for disability, and she was initially denied. At the time, I did not know too much about the disability determination process, but I had worked as a disability paralegal for 12 months, and at least knew about how age and education affected decisions. So, I told my mom she should reapply when she was 54 years and 9 months. That would give the examiner 90 days to gather the info and make "a better decision" so that when she turned 55 she would qualify and already be approved for benefits.

Well the new examiner still denied the claim, at which time I put my name on the claim as my mom's authorized representative as we filed an application for reconsideration. I was living in another state at the time and this would allow me to be copied on everything happening with the claim. So immediately at reconsideration, I sent a statement explaining how far my mom had gone in school, what the physical exertional level of her last job was (medium level), and what her doctors had said about her inability to continue doing medium level work with her heart condition.

My mom's claim was approved shortly thereafter with no new medical evidence required.

The only glitch that I can assume caused my "54.9 year plan" to fail initially was that my mom must have gotten an inexperienced claims examiner who was not able to put all the pieces of the puzzle together. So I had to help him.

Reconsideration examiners are generally more experienced examiners so s/he may have done the right thing even without my letter. Still, knowing all you can about the disability determination process gives you the power to help inexperienced adjudicators make "a better decision".

Action Step 8: When you receive your *Notice of Decision*, whether it is an approval or denial, please read it carefully, reviewing the disability onset date, or reasons for denial. Both can give you clues on how to proceed when you use the information contained in this Step.

STEP 9:
WHAT TO DO IF YOUR CLAIM IS DENIED

If your initial claim application for Social Security Disability benefits or SSI benefits is denied, and you believe that you are disabled from working your past job or any job, then you should file for reconsideration or an appeal, depending on what level of the process you are.

In the *Notice of Decision letter*, there should be a brochure that explains the timelines for filing for reconsideration or an appeal. Be sure to file for the reconsideration, ALJ hearing or Appeal as soon as possible. You will be surprised how quickly that time will slip away if you do not act on it right away.

Filing for reconsideration on a denial decision or an appeal versus just filing a new application can mean thousands of dollars in retroactive benefits to you if your claim is later approved. So you should read the brochure and follow all instructions to allow for a timely appeal application.

If you read the clues included in your "*Notice of Decision*" letter as outlined in Step 8, you will be able to assess just how far you will have to go to eventually land a positive outcome.

Denials based on an assessment of "non-severe" have the greatest chance of repeat denials, and in my opinion are not worth pursuing. Denials based on "can do other work" will be the easiest to pursue and win because you only have one more hurdle to cross, i.e. you only have to prove that there are no other jobs out there that you can do, given your physical or mental limitations.

Getting Help with Your Appeal

When should you start to look for a professional or a disability advocate to help you with your claim?

That is a good question, and the answer depends on your temperament as well as how the disability professionals operate in your locality.

If you are extremely nervous about the process, you might consider beginning your search for an attorney or disability paralegal after you have received your first denial. You may or may not be able to find a local attorney who will do any work on your case prior to your Administrative Law Judge hearing or appeals level, or after you have received a denial on your reconsideration.

From an examiner's perspective, I can tell you that having an attorney at the reconsideration level—unless you have a mental disability—does not really influence the decision. This is because you are essentially dealing with the same group of people who processed your initial denial. They are all trained the same way, and unless you have new medical evidence that is somewhat different from the old, you will more than likely get a similar decision.

At the higher appeals levels, however, your claim leaves the hands of the DDS office and is placed in the hands of an Administrative Law Judge (ALJ) for review or the Courts. The ALJ has more discretion than examiners do in deciding your claim, and you can actually be seen by the ALJ during the hearing, unlike the situation with the examiner and medical consultant staff who will never see you at the initial or reconsideration levels.

Another reason to consider holding off on getting an attorney until after your reconsideration denial is that you will get to keep all your back/retroactive benefits if your claim is approved at this stage. This is more than a little deal because attorneys typically can charged you 25% of back benefits, up to a maximum of $6000 to represent you in the claim.

As an examiner, I used to loathe seeing claimants being represented at the initial application level who had medical conditions that were obviously going to be an allowance. But, in claims alleging a mental disability, having a representative was extremely beneficial because these persons serve as relay messengers and helped to get claimants through the process.

Does Having an Attorney Increase Your Chances of Receiving Disability Benefits?

There are statistics that show having an attorney increases a claimant's chance of receiving benefits, but I think it refers to having an attorney at the ALJ and Appeals level, not at initial or reconsideration levels.

Whether a claimant had an attorney listed on his application never influenced my decision on a claim or altered the process in any way. While notices were sent to attorneys or representatives in addition to the claimant, that was basically the only difference, and that was done automatically if a certain form was in the file.

Consider Finding an Attorney If You Have Any of These Conditions

You should certainly consider getting an attorney or representative as soon as possible if you have a mental impairment, just because your representative can assist you in taking care of routine matters. In addition, if you suffer from Chronic Fatigue Syndrome or Fibromyalgia, or have issues with disabling pain due to any cause other than a structural abnormality, you should try to find a representative at the earliest possible time to help you present your evidence in the most favorable way.

Attorneys are Good to Obtain Immediately after You Get Your Reconsideration Denial

Other than those scenarios described above, you should consider getting an attorney the moment you have received your reconsideration denial letter, i.e. after SSA has denied your claim two times: at initial application and at reconsideration. That is when your attorney will have the most opportunity to shine and to help you shine as you prepare to go before an Administrative Law Judge.

Talking to an attorney after you get your reconsideration denial letter is a good idea for another reason as well. It is a good screening mechanism. Since attorneys only get paid if they help you win your claim, they are not likely to accept claims that do not have some chance of winning. So if they accept your claim, it is a good indication that your condition is at least a severe one, and somewhat winnable.

How to Find a Disability Attorney and Reduce Fees Simultaneously

Social Security Disability attorneys can easily be found in the yellow pages. They also advertise on late night television where I live. And a good thing about SS disability claims is that attorneys accept cases on a contingency fee basis, which means if they are not successful in proving your disability, you do not have to pay their fee.

Claims ESP Disability Directory

If you are looking for a disability representative or attorney, and do not know where to start, you might find the service we offer useful.

We prescreen disability representatives based on their experience, their success rate in representing claimants, their ability to connect with you in a timely matter, and their willingness to give you a free evaluation on your claim. Visit our directory here:

http://www.directory.social-security-disability.com

National Organization of Social Security Claimant Representatives

Another organization I am familiar with which you might want to consider contacting if you need an attorney or disability representative is the National Organization of Social Security Claimant Representatives (NOSSCR.org). They have a lawyer referral service that may be useful. What I like about them is that they have annual conferences, which allow the members to stay updated on new social security disability laws, policies and regulations, and they advocate for the rights of disabled claimants as a matter of course.

Disability Advocates

Disability Advocates is another organization you may want to consider. They provide legal representation as well as advocacy services for Social Security Disability claimants. You can check to see if they have a representative available to assist you in your area. Online at: http://disability-advocate.com/

Prepaid Legal Services

Finally, if you want to find a competent attorney and save on the amount of money you pay in fees if you win your claim, you could check out Pre-Paid Legal Services. This is a national organization, with attorneys in every state, which does for attorney services what your health insurance coverage does for medical services, i.e. they make retaining an attorney affordable by charging a reasonable monthly fee for participation.

But the reason I recommend paying their monthly membership fee – which can start as low as $17 -- is that as a member you can qualify for a reduction in their contingency fees by 5%. This means that if they handle your disability claim, and win it for you, you will end up paying only 20% of your back benefits instead of the standard 25% that most attorneys charge.

But what does that mean in real money terms? Let's say they win your disability claim and SSA owes you $16,000 in back benefits. (*Note: this is not an unrealistic figure, given the time it takes for a reconsideration and bringing your claim before an Administrative Law Judge*). A regular attorney would receive 25% of that amount, or $4000, but with a Pre-Paid Legal Services disability attorney, you would only be paying the attorney 20% of $16,000, or $3200. So you would save $800, and get to keep that extra $800 in your pocket when your claim is settled.

So, even if you are paying a monthly membership fee of $17 per month, you can see that you still come out ahead because not only will you have saved $800 on your SS disability case, but you will have access to an attorney for any other type of legal matter you might encounter throughout the process. Their telephone consultation services are free with your membership, and they will also write a letter on your behalf for many legal matters you face, and sometimes a letter will keep a small matter from escalating into a big one.

Beyond that, as a person who has lived off $300 a month income for more months than I care to admit, I find that even though I maintained no health insurance coverage, I always maintained my Pre-Paid Legal insurance coverage, no matter what.

Why? Because having served in public service programs for many years, I know that people who are poor, disabled or otherwise in financial straits are often the victims of something or another, and have a host of concerns that they often need legal advice to resolve. Whether it be issues with housing--facing evictions--or mortgages--facing foreclosures--or any other legal issue, you are covered. You have an attorney just a phone call away for a reasonable monthly fee. They also prepare your will for free with your sign up, if requested.

So even though I am one that keeps a Pre-Paid Legal Services attorney on my payroll through the thick and thin of my finances, having a low cost membership makes good sense for anyone who thinks they will need an attorney in the near future.

You will not only get a discounted fee rate when an attorney from their reputable law firm handles your disability claim, but you will have them at your beck and call, literally, to consult with for any other legal matter that may surface during this stressful time.

If interested, you can learn more about what they offer, and you can check out their affordable membership plans at **www.prepaidlegal.com**. If you would like me to work with you personally to set up your account, please contact me directly or reference "associate ID 119658540" when you enroll and I will contact you.

Action Step 9: If your reconsideration claim is denied, consider contacting an attorney for a free consultation to see if the attorney/firm will accept your claim. If they say yes, it is a good indication that your medical condition is a severe one. Our directory service is at www.directory.social-security-disability-esp.com to sign up online.

Remember, if you believe, suspect or know that you are disabled from working, then you should read the brochure that came with your Notice of Decision denial letter and follow the instructions noted on how to file for a reconsideration or appeal. **Do this within the timelines specified in the brochure.**

This is particularly important in SSI claims because if you do not file for an appeal in a timely matter and you later decide just to reapply for benefits, you will forfeit your right to get disability benefits as of the date of your original initial application. This could mean the potential loss of hundreds or thousands of dollars in payments, if your subsequent application is approved.

Contact an attorney or disability paralegal or advocate if you think you will need help in presenting your claim at appeal. Their fees are contingent on them winning your claim, so you have nothing to lose in consulting with one about your claim.

Still, whether you have located a representative to help you or not, do not let that deadline for filing your appeal go by. You can let SSA know you want an appeal by the deadline date, while you continue to search for a legal representative to assist you.

HOW TO GET ON
SSA'S VIP CLAIM LIST

Let me preface this chapter by saying that disability examiners, for the most part, are given full flexibility in managing their own caseloads. For this reason they have to be very organized and efficient, and usually have to develop a system for keeping their cases in order, so that decisions are processed on a "first one in, first one out" basis. This assumes that if all the information is in the file to make a case decision on a claim, that the decision is made in the order of who applied first, or which claim is the oldest.

However, sometimes-particular claims do move to the top of the list. This includes claims that are obviously going to be approvals based on the extreme severity of a claimant's impairments. Claims where it is determined that a claimant's condition is terminal will get preferential treatment.

As alluded to previously, if an examiner has a stack of claims ready for a decision, and those claims are placed in two stacks, i.e. allowances and denials, the examiner will process the approvals first. "What's the rush in delivering bad news" might be part of the logic for doing approvals first.

One might assume that claims where an applicant has been granted "Presumptive Disability benefits would be a claim that moved to the top of the list, but this is not necessarily so. The examiner's logic is that "this claimant is already receiving monthly benefits for up to six months, so there is no need to rush inputting a decision."

All the above situations, in my opinion, are somewhat justified. Those who have severe disabilities should get their claims approved at the earliest possible time. However, there is one other situation that will put a claim at the top of the list, not just in rendering the final decision, but in all phases of the disability decision-making process.

Regrettably, preferential treatment rendered in the situation that I am about to reveal is purely predicated on politics--again, this is in my opinion--not whether the claimant has a severe impairment or not.

I hesitated to even include it here for obvious reasons, i.e. it makes my blood boil. To me it makes a mockery of the system and is an abuse of the system; still, if you are down to your last resort and need to get some preferential treatment, this may help you.

What is it? What is this thing that might help you as a claimant get the best decision in the absolute least amount of time?

Well, first you must make contact with your Congressman or his staff, and then convince someone in his / her office to call DDS on your behalf. Once DDS gets that call, the time clock begins. Examiners by way of their supervisor's instructions, by way of their supervisor's manager's instructions, and on and on, are expected to make that claim a priority.

It is the only type case where examiners have to keep their supervisors abreast of its progress. It is the only type case where I deliberately tried to delay a decision just because of the sheer mockery of the system that it represented. To me it said: "Those who have power are always trying to walk over those who don't." Where is the justice? It means those who are extremely disabled have to wait on a decision because the examiner is forced to spend time on a case that is sometimes borderline at best. In fact in one of those congressional aide intervention cases, the decision of the examiner and the medical consultant was disregarded, albeit subtly, and an approval was allowed when it would have otherwise been a denial.

Anyway, let me get off my soapbox because that is not the purpose of giving you this tip. What I am trying to say is that if you have not been able to get through to your state DDS office or feel that they have mistreated you or not been responsive to your needs, this is absolutely one of the quickest ways to get the attention you feel you deserve. So go ahead, contact your congressional representative's office and make your case, and good luck to you!.

SUMMARY

Getting regular Social Security Disability Insurance or SSI benefits when you are disabled is a process that can be complicated when you do not know what to expect.

But this 9 Step guide has hopefully shown you the important things that you could do to increase your chance of receiving benefits by providing the exact information that your claims examiners and medical consultants will need to assess your disabilities and to decide your claim.

If you remember only one thing from the 9 Steps, remember to use the language of function in all your communications to and with the examiner about your disabilities.

Step 2 and Step 5 give you specific terms to use when speaking or writing of your work functions and limitations, whether you are alleging a mental or physical disability. If you, your medical doctor or other collateral sources all use this language of function – specifically mentioning those functions that are needed and related to the work environment – then it will be easier for the examiners and medical consultants to reach an accurate decision on your disability, since everyone will be speaking the same language.

Getting disability payments that you are entitled to can make your financial life much easier to manage. It allows you to concentrate on other things in your life that need attention, and removes much of the stress and worry about providing for your own basic needs when you are no longer able to work.

For these reasons, you should review the 9 Steps to getting disability benefits at different stages of the disability process. It will be a reminder to you to keep emphasizing to the examiner what basic work related functions you can no longer do as a result of your impairments.

It should also remind you to keep checking on the status of your claim so that it does not get lost in the stack of all the claims your examiner is managing on a day-to-day basis. By periodically checking on your claim, you will get a faster decision on your claim. It does not matter if you know the right questions to ask or if you ad lib, because in disability claims, the squeaky wheel really does get the oil.

Best wishes to you as you move forward with your claim.

ONLINE RESOURCES

Social Security Disability Examiner Speaks Plainly:

- Free Disability Evaluation at www.directory.social-security-disability-esp.com

- Social Security Disability Claims ESP Home—Here is our main site featuring an ex Social Security Disability Claims Examiner giving tips on getting favorable Disability Insurance Benefits & SSI decisions. http://social-security-disability-esp.com or http://bit.ly/disabilityespmain

- Free Disability Newsletter--Free Social Security Disability Newsletter -- Claims ESP—a former Disability Examiner (DE) gives tips on getting your Social Security Disability Insurance Benefits and SSI decisions reviewed timely and accurately. Information on forms, PD, medical doctors, attorneys and more. Sign up for your free copy now at http://social-security-disability-esp.com/Free_Newsletter.html or http://bit.ly/nl-claimsesp

- 9 Steps Disability Blog--Stay up to date on what happening at Social Security Disability ESP with this blog. Find out when new articles are added to the site to help you win your disability claim. http://social-security-disability-esp.com/9steps

Reference Articles:

- *First Impressions: What a Claims Examiner Determines About Your Adult Social Security Disability or Supplemental Security Income Claim in the First 15 Minutes* http://www.9steps.social-security-disability-esp.com/First-15-Minutes.html

- Five Step Sequential Evaluation Process in Disability Determination http://www.9steps.social-security-disability-esp.com/SSA-Five-Step-Sequential-Evaluation.html

Recommended Reading

Nolo's Guide to Social Security Disability: Getting & Keeping Your Benefits, David Morton, MD.

This guide is one of my favorites, and a must have for anyone dealing with the SSA. *The Wall Street Journal* had this to say about this title:

 "A thorough analysis and discussion of the requirements to qualify for Social Security disability benefits. The author is a physician who was formerly a chief medical consultant for the Social Security Administration."

Direct Amazon link: http://amzn.to/nologuide

More Disability Reading Recommendations here:

http://social-security-disability-esp.com/Books.html

Affordable Legal Services

- Pre-Paid Legal Services does for attorneys what medical insurance does for doctors--i.e. it places services within the reach of those who need it, at an affordable monthly fee. While attorneys handling disability claims do so on a contingency fee basis, only being paid if they win your claim, your Pre-Paid Legal Services membership allows you to receive contingency fee-based services at a 5% saving off the standard rate charged by most attorneys. Plus, you get unlimited telephone consultations on any legal matter you're facing, and will preparation comes free with your membership. Get a reputable disability attorney from a reputable law firm in your state working for you on your claim as soon as you sign up!

  If interested, you can learn more about what they offer, and you can check out their affordable membership plans at www.prepaidlegal.com. If you would like me to work with you personally to set up your account, please contact me directly through the contact information located at www.social-security-disability-esp.com, or reference "associate ID 119658540" when you enroll.

ABOUT THE AUTHOR

Loretta Crosby is an ex Social Security Disability claims examiner, having worked in the states of Georgia and North Carolina. During her tenure with the North Carolina Disability Determination Service, an organization that provides disability decisions as a contractual arm of the Social Security Administration, she was certified as a "Single Decision Maker" which granted her the ability to decide certain claims alleging physical disabilities without the input of a medical consultant.

Prior to becoming a disability adjudicator, Crosby served as an overseas volunteer for the Bahá'í Faith for over five years in Haifa, Israel and Accra, Ghana (West Africa).

A native South Carolinian, Crosby grew up in Brooklyn, NY. Her professional career includes a range of public service positions. As a social service generalist, she certified clients for Aid to Families with Dependent Children, Food Stamps and Medicaid. As a social service analyst, she worked with Day Care Center providers to ensure low income children received nutritious meals through the Child Care Food Program administered by USDA. She has also served as a county Child Protective Services caseworker determining issues of child abuse and neglect, and helping families access treatment services when indicated.

Crosby holds a BS degree in psychology, and was an award-winning newspaper journalist while covering health, education, welfare and religious issues at a Knight-Ridder newspaper in Georgia. Internationally, she has served as an assistant editor of a global religious bi-weekly news bulletin, and as editor of a national news magazine in Israel and Ghana, respectively.

"Though I still do not know what I want to be when I grow up, my passion has always been to assist people to overcome obstacles that stand in the way of them realizing their full God-given potential," Crosby said.

"Sometimes those stumbling blocks involve economic challenges and sometimes they involve a lack of faith in the abilities of their Father to change their circumstances, or otherwise impact outcomes in a positive way."

Crosby says she seeks to "serve, bless, inspire and live on purpose!"

"My adopted motto is 'Pray as if everything depended on God -- and then act as if everything depended on you.'"

Crosby is an independent content writer, web-designer and info-preneur. Catch her online at RecallingHealth.com, SheaButterCenter.com and Social-Security-Disability-ESP.com. Tweet her at twitter.com/onepupil9.